THE DOPAMINE CODE WORKBOOK

THE DOPAMINE CODE WORKBOOK

Your Guided Companion for Unlocking Habits to Boost Happiness and Productivity

DR. SYDNEY CERUTO

Founder and CEO of MindLAB Neuroscience

ADAMS MEDIA

NEW YORK AMSTERDAM/ANTWERP LONDON TORONTO

SYDNEY/MELBOURNE NEW DELHI

adamsmedia

Adams Media
An Imprint of Simon & Schuster, LLC
100 Technology Center Drive
Stoughton, MA 02072

The authorized representative in the EEA is Simon & Schuster Nederland B.V., Herculesplein 96, 3584 AA Utrecht, Netherlands. info@simonandschuster.nl

First Adams Media trade paperback edition October 2026

ADAMS MEDIA and colophon are registered trademarks of Simon & Schuster, LLC.

Interior design by Colleen Cunningham

Manufactured in the United States of America

1 2026

ISBN 978-1-5072-2627-8

Dedicated to you, the reader,
for trusting what your brain was trying to tell you,
and for being brave enough to listen.

What follows will not always feel easy.

Some exercises will click immediately.

Others will take repetition, patience, and a few false starts.

That is not failure.

That is your nervous system learning a new language.

Acknowledgments

To Lindsey Smith, my fabulous agent, for her belief in this project and her tireless work behind the scenes to make it happen.

To Brit Smith, for championing this companion workbook and seeing its potential from the start.

To Sarah Doughty, for her sharp editorial eye and thoughtful guidance in shaping every exercise into something clear, practical, and genuinely useful.

Contents

Introduction

Have you ever looked forward to reaching a big goal, only to feel dissatisfied once you achieved it? Do you find yourself constantly craving novelty, even enjoying the chase more than the reward itself? Does the pull of social media feeds and message notifications make it difficult for you to stay present in moments with friends and family? If this sounds familiar, you are not alone.

Dopamine is your brain's central engine for motivation, learning, and lasting change. It pushes you to pursue goals, form new habits, and overcome obstacles, even when the odds are steep. But when technology, work, and stress hijack this motivator, you can end up stuck in loops of craving, distraction, and burnout. Fortunately, you don't need to remain stuck in these loops: You can redesign your habits and environment so your brain works *for* you, rather than *against* you.

The Dopamine Code Workbook is your easy-to-follow hands-on companion for making this shift. Through six chapters of exploring your own habits, as well as simple practices, you will map your day through its highs and lows in dopamine, build a personalized "Dopamine Menu" for lasting satisfaction, and make realistic changes to your everyday life. All you need is something to write with and a willingness to try out small adjustments.

The exercises that follow will translate the science of your brain into concrete results you can feel in your daily life, boosting energy, focus, and satisfaction. You'll:

- Identify what motivates you.
- Try a personalized dopamine detox.
- Create your own menu of fulfilling habits.
- Make device-free zones and rituals for balanced dopamine.
- And more.

Before jumping into these exercises, be sure to read through the next sections on dopamine basics and best practices for this workbook. Here, you'll dig a little deeper into the science of dopamine, along with the details for making the most of each exercise. With this understanding of how dopamine acts and how to work through the following chapters, you'll be ready to take action.

By the end of this workbook, you'll have a stronger understanding of what makes you tick, what gives you drive and pleasure, and what you can do to bring more happiness, productivity, and satisfaction to your life. Your journey to dopamine mastery starts here; turn the page and let's begin.

What Is Dopamine?

Scientifically speaking, dopamine is a neurotransmitter: a chemical messenger produced in specific regions of your brain in response to anticipated or received reward. The released dopamine helps regulate movement, motivation, reward, learning, and emotional responses. It allows nerve cells to communicate with one another so you can anticipate rewards, make decisions, and update your behavior based on what you have learned over time. When dopamine is released, it strengthens the pathways that say, "This mattered—remember it, and do it again."

What makes dopamine especially powerful is that it responds not only to rewards themselves, but also to your brain's predictions about those rewards. Dopamine often rises when you expect something good to happen and when the outcome is better than expected. It can drop when things fall short. This is what keeps you seeking, striving, and adjusting course. It fuels the energy of wanting and pursuit far more than the quiet feeling of liking or contentment. This distinction matters, because it explains why you can chase a promotion, a relationship, or a big purchase with intense focus and still feel oddly flat once you get it. Dopamine drove the pursuit, but it does not guarantee deep satisfaction.

Often called the "pleasure molecule," dopamine is designed to keep you wanting: Evolutionarily, craving is what kept your ancestors alive. Because of dopamine, they were driven to hunt, gather, make shelter, and do all of the other things crucial to survival. Today, dopamine drives you similarly to pursue everything from good food to workplace achievements.

When you understand that dopamine is a molecule of craving built into your DNA, you can let go of any judgments you might have toward yourself for feeling restless or unsatisfied in life. You can begin to see that your brain is simply doing its job. Luckily, this job doesn't need to get in the way of a life of true satisfaction and happiness. You can work with dopamine to lean into what brings deeper contentment, and make changes to what might not be serving you.

Ultimately, healthy dopamine function is about balance and calibration, not about chasing constant highs. When dopamine signaling is overstimulated or depleted, your motivation can swing between restless craving and complete shutdown. When it is in balance, you are able to feel motivated, curious, and engaged by everyday life.

How to Use This Book

This book is a step-by-step guide to understanding and reshaping your dopamine system, where each chapter builds on the one before it. For this reason, it is best to move in order from Chapter 1 through Chapter 6, and in the specific order of the exercises in each chapter. In Chapter 1, you'll uncover your current dopamine patterns. In Chapter 2, you'll lower the noise of overstimulation. In Chapter 3, you'll support your brain through sleep, movement, light, and intentional spaces. In Chapter 4, you'll rebuild your Dopamine Menu with healthier sources of reward. Chapter 5 applies the work you've done in Chapters 1–4 to improve focus, flow, and creativity. Finally, Chapter 6 anchors everything you've learned to connection, resilience, and meaning.

Within each chapter, the exercises are the real engine of change. Start with the exercise's short introduction, then follow the steps and finish the exercise by reading the information on why this practice is an important part of bringing your dopamine into balance and finding satisfaction in everyday life.

You do not need to complete every exercise in a chapter in one sitting; it is far more powerful to choose a realistic pace and stick with it. The exercises will have more room to sink in and you will be better able to stay the course rather than get overwhelmed. A good rule of thumb is to complete one to three exercises per week, using the time in between to notice what is shifting in your mood, energy, and behavior.

Importantly, treat this book as a space for discovery, not a test. You are not looking to get some "perfect score"; you are trying things out in your own life, learning from what you observe, and adjusting as you go. You can circle back to earlier chapters whenever your circumstances change or you want a refresher. Over time, repeating exercises will allow you to see the bigger picture of your progress.

The goal through this workbook is not to rush to the end but to slowly shift how your brain responds to reward so that motivation and satisfaction become more stable, sustainable parts of your everyday experience. Simply pick up a pen or pencil and turn the page to get started.

CHAPTER 1

Understanding What Drives Your Dopamine System

For decades, pop culture has sold a seductive but ultimately misleading story: that dopamine is the chemical source of your happiness. But as you learned earlier in this book, neuroscience reveals a much more nuanced truth about its ties to craving, motivation, and the relentless pursuit of more.

This chapter is not about reading more theory; it is about getting to the bottom of how dopamine impacts *your* everyday life. Through the following exercises, you are going to map the landscape of your own brain. You will actively track the gap between "wanting" something and truly "liking" it once you have it, and you will pinpoint exactly where your dopamine system is being overstimulated. By identifying what sparks your motivation and what your patterns of high and low stimulation look like, you can stop fighting a losing battle against your own biology. Instead, you'll start building the understanding you need to master dopamine—and live a truly satisfying life.

Map Your Dopamine Day

Start by taking a closer look at how dopamine shows up in an ordinary day. In this activity, you will notice when you feel energized, restless, flat, or pulled toward quick hits of stimulation.

1 **List the main activities you do in a typical day.** Include work, screens used, meals, movement, social time, and "in-between" moments like scrolling in bed or snacking while stressed:

2 **For each activity, note how it feels in the moment.** Ask yourself if each activity feels energizing, numbing, comforting, anxious, calming, or overstimulating, and note that feeling beside the activity in Step 1.

3 **Now, notice how you feel after each activity.** For each one, write a few words about how you feel thirty to sixty minutes later. For example, you might feel proud, worn out, restless, satisfied, guilty, or hungry for more.

4 Circle one activity that gives you a boost of dopamine in the moment but leaves you feeling worse afterward. In the space provided, write about this activity: What draws you to it, even if you know you will feel worse afterward? How does your body feel both during and after the activity? How is your mood both during and after the activity?

WHY THIS EXERCISE **MATTERS**

Large boosts of dopamine feel beneficial in the moment. Unfortunately, they often quietly drain energy, focus, and satisfaction later. By noticing the difference between how something feels during a specific moment and afterward, you begin to see that dopamine is driving you toward quick relief instead of long-term fulfillment. Awareness is the first step in reshaping your motivation. ■

Identify What Motivates You

Dopamine does not just respond to rewards. It also responds to cues. These are the sights, sounds, places, and feelings that signal a reward might be coming. In this exercise, you will identify what cues tend to trigger a motivated boost of dopamine and what cues tend to shut it down.

1 **Recall three recent moments when you felt genuinely motivated.** Were you answering emails efficiently? Starting a workout? Cooking a meal? Maybe tackling a project? Once you have written down the moment, think back to what led up to that motivation. Did you see a good-looking recipe on TV that made you want to start cooking? Did a phone call with a friend make you feel excited about working out?

Moment of Motivation #1	Moment of Motivation #2	Moment of Motivation #3

2 Now recall three moments when you felt stuck, numb, or resistant to getting things done. Times you procrastinated, avoided a task, or simply shut down. Once you've written each moment, think back to what happened before you felt that resistance. Did you struggle to fall asleep the previous night? Were you scrolling through social media for longer than you might have planned?

Moment of Resistance #1	Moment of Resistance #2	Moment of Resistance #3

3 Compare your lists. What patterns do you notice about what sparks your motivation versus what shuts it down? Are there specific environments (like an office space), people (like a certain coworker), thoughts (like "I am already behind"), or times of day (like the start of the morning) that consistently boost dopamine—or not? Use the following space to reflect on these questions.

WHY THIS EXERCISE **MATTERS**

Dopamine is highly sensitive to cues that suggest a reward—or something less appealing—is coming. Certain cues can keep you stuck in a habit without you even realizing it. Luckily, when you see your own patterns, you can begin to design your day around triggers that naturally wake up your motivation. You can also gently reduce or reshape the cues that lead to shutdown and avoidance. Instead of blaming yourself for "laziness," you learn to work with the biology of your dopamine system. ■

Distinguish Wanting from Liking

It is easy to assume that if you crave something intensely, you will enjoy it just as much once you have it. However, this is often not the case. This exercise helps you separate the dopamine-driven "urge" for something from the actual experience of satisfaction upon receiving it.

1 **Identify three recent rewards you pursued very actively.** These could be a purchase you researched for weeks, a specific food you craved, a social interaction you chased, or a professional milestone you worked toward.

Reward #1	Reward #2	Reward #3

2 **Rate the feelings of wanting versus liking.** For each listed item, rate how much you craved it before you received it, and how much you enjoyed it when you actually had it. Ratings are from 1 to 10, with 1 being very little to no craving and 10 being the most intense.

Reward #1		Reward #2		Reward #3	
Wanting Score:	Liking Score:	Wanting Score:	Liking Score:	Wanting Score:	Liking Score:

3 **Explore the difference between how much you wanted something and how much you enjoyed it once you had it.** Look back at the reward with the most significant difference between the Wanting Score and the Liking Score. What did the anticipation feel like compared to the reality? Did the "high" fade immediately? Did you feel let down? Did you immediately start looking for the next thing?

4 **Reflect on the "why."** For the reward where the Liking Score was the lowest compared to the Wanting Score, dig deeper into what propelled you to crave that reward. What was the driving force? Was it for genuine joy? The fear of missing out on something others had? A desire to relieve some stress? Use this space to reflect on the answer.

WHY THIS EXERCISE **MATTERS**

Recognizing the gap between what your brain promised and what reality delivered is an important step toward breaking the cycle of endless chasing after rewards. When you see that big cravings lead to unpredictable outcomes (i.e., you may not feel real joy), you can stop following every impulse and start choosing rewards that actually deliver satisfaction. ■

Explore Where Uncertainty Hooks You

Dopamine spikes highest when a reward is unpredictable. This is why checking your phone, refreshing your email, or watching the news can become a compulsive habit. The brain is looking for the "maybe." This exercise helps you identify instances in your life where you seek out the dopamine rush of uncertainty.

1 **List three compulsive habits where you frequently check for updates.** Examples include refreshing social media, checking stock prices, looking at message notifications, scanning news headlines, or checking dating apps.

1.

2.

3.

2 Describe the physical sensation of the "check."

Before you check for an update, what does that urge feel like in your body? Does your chest feel tight? Do you feel a buzzing energy inside? A restless twitch?

What happens to that feeling if you don't find anything new (the disappointment of "no reward")?

3 **Create certainty.** To counterbalance the anxiety of the "maybe," plan one activity today that has a 100% guaranteed reward and is under your control. This could be drinking a perfect cup of tea, taking a warm bath, reading a chapter of a favorite book, or doing a specific stretch.

My certainty for today is:

How I felt afterward:

WHY THIS EXERCISE **MATTERS**

Life is filled with unpredictabilities that keep your dopamine system permanently revved up and anxious. By consciously engaging in activities that focus on specific, stable outcomes, you signal to your brain that it is safe to deactivate the "seeking" mechanism of constantly anticipating what lies ahead, and engage the "enjoying" mechanism of real pleasure in what lies in front of you. ■

Find Your Stimulation Sweet Spot

Your dopamine system—and your body as a whole—functions best on a certain level of stimulation. Too little stimulation, and you feel bored and unmotivated. Too much stimulation, and you feel overwhelmed and anxious. This exercise helps you identify what amount of stimulation is best for you and recognize when you have entered a danger zone of overindulgence or boredom.

1 **Track your stimulation for three days.** List everything that makes you feel stimulated: work tasks, social media use, food, entertainment, social interaction, exercise intensity, caffeine, news consumption, and online shopping. Include the time you typically spent on each.

DAY 1	DAY 2	DAY 3

2 **Rate how stimulated you were each day, and how elevated your energy level and mood were.** You can use a rating of 1 for low and 5 for high, or just note "low," "medium," or "high"—whatever works best for you.

DAY 1	DAY 2	DAY 3
Stimulation level: Energy and mood: Quality of sleep: Notes:	Stimulation level: Energy and mood: Quality of sleep: Notes:	Stimulation level: Energy and mood: Quality of sleep: Notes:

3 **Identify what overstimulation is for you.** Overstimulation means lower energy and mood, so look back at the days when your energy and mood were rated the lowest. How did the stimulation for that day compare to the days when you had more energy or a better mood? Did you spend extra time on social media? Did you have more work meetings? Did you spend more time reading or watching the news? Did you eat more guilty-pleasure foods? Reflect in the space provided.

4 **Describe what overstimulation feels like in your body and mind.** When you have crossed into overstimulation, what physical sensations do you notice? Tension? Restlessness? Mental fog? Emotional flatness? An overall sense of being numb? Record your response in the space provided.

5 **Now think of a time when you felt flat, unmotivated, or emotionally numb—when nothing seemed worth pursuing.** What were the circumstances? What did you reach for to try to feel something? Reflect here:

WHY THIS EXERCISE **MATTERS**

Most people continue to seek stimulation even after they've reached their sweet spot because they cannot distinguish between "energized" and "overstimulated." Under-stimulation is the opposite trap: When your environment lacks novelty, challenge, or meaning, dopamine activity drops and the brain responds with apathy, emotional flatness, or compulsive novelty-seeking. People in this state often describe feeling "stuck" or "going through the motions." By tuning into your body's signals, you can catch yourself before you reach burnout, numbness, apathy, and more. ■

Find Out What "Enough" Means for You

The concept of "enough" is radically different from the concept of "more." "Enough" is the point where you are satisfied, motivated, and engaged—before your dopamine system tips into overstimulation. This exercise teaches you to identify when you are satisfied so you can intentionally stop seeking more before the pleasure fades.

1. **Identify one activity that you typically overdo.** This is something you enjoy but often continue doing past the point where the enjoyment peaks. Examples include scrolling through social media, eating past fullness, staying at a party too long, or working on a project when you are already worn out.

2. **Experiment with satisfaction.** Engage in the activity you identified and pay close attention to your pleasure level every five minutes. Note the moment when pleasure peaks. Then continue engaging in the activity for another five to ten minutes. Note when joy stops going up, and when it starts to decline.

Peak pleasure occurred ____ minutes into the activity.

I continued for an additional ____ minutes.

3 Reflect on the experiment. Use these prompts to deeply think about your experience:

I noticed the enjoyment dropping off when:

How I felt about continuing past the point where I felt the most enjoyment:

How I felt as I continued:

How I felt after:

4 **Create a stopping point.** Based on your experiment, define the moment when you will intentionally stop this activity in the future. Will you set a timer? Will you watch for a specific signal (like the first moment of restlessness or the beginning of a yawn)? Plan out when and how you will stop in the space provided.

5 **Reflect on resistance.** The concept of stopping at "enough" often triggers internal resistance. Your brain expected more, and so now you may experience restlessness, FOMO, or a nagging sense of incompleteness. What comes up for you? Is it a fear of missing out? Feeling deprived? Trying to get the most out of your investment? Write honestly about what makes stopping at "enough" feel difficult, so you can take the first step toward overcoming those roadblocks.

WHY THIS EXERCISE **MATTERS**

Learning to stop before the dopamine high becomes a dopamine low is one of the most powerful ways to recalibrate your dopamine system. Each time you honor what is truly "enough," you train your brain to embrace sustainable satisfaction. Over time, this rewires your nervous system to seek quality pleasure rather than quantity stimulation. ■

Distinguish Low Dopamine from Burnout and Adaptation

One important question to ask yourself when dopamine is imbalanced is whether it is low dopamine, burnout, or adaptation that is the cause. Low dopamine is reduced drive and motivation from genuine depletion. It can stem from poor sleep, nutritional deficiency, grief, or underlying health conditions. Burnout, meanwhile, is a dopamine system overload from sustained output without recovery. Your brain has been running at full capacity for too long and the reward system has gone offline to protect itself. You feel exhausted, cynical, and detached. Finally, adaptation is when your dopamine receptors have become overstimulated and now need more and more intensity to feel the same satisfaction that was once felt. The difference: Burnout and adaptation are caused by too much. Low dopamine signaling is caused by not enough of the right inputs. This exercise helps you distinguish the three for yourself, so you can better understand what your dopamine system is in need of in the moment.

1 **Describe a recent time when you felt unmotivated, flat, or apathetic.** What were you doing (or not doing) during this time? How long did it last?

2 **Now ask yourself: Which of these was true?** Check all that apply.

Low Dopamine:

- ☐ I was sleep deprived.
- ☐ I had poor nutrition.
- ☐ I was genuinely uninterested in what I was being asked to do.
- ☐ I was experiencing depression or another mental health condition.

Burnout:

- [ ] I had been pushing hard for weeks or months before I felt flat.
- [ ] I was experiencing chronic stress, anxiety, or interpersonal conflict.
- [ ] I had not taken meaningful time off or allowed myself true recovery time for months.
- [ ] I felt emotionally numb, cynical, or detached from work or relationships that used to matter to me.

Adaptation:

- [ ] I had been using a stimulating activity (social media, gaming, shopping) heavily and then stopped.
- [ ] I had achieved a big goal prior.
- [ ] Things I used to enjoy stopped feeling rewarding. I needed more intensity to feel the same satisfaction.

3 Based on your checklist, reflect on what was actually happening. Were you perhaps experiencing burnout (from overwork), adaptation (from overstimulation), emotional flatness (from achieving but not feeling satisfied), or a sign that something needed to change? Be specific.

4 If your lack of motivation was due to adaptation (your brain becoming less responsive), what had you feeling overstimulated? Social media? Work? Physical activity? Substances? Write honestly about what might have caused your dopamine receptors to downregulate.

WHY THIS EXERCISE **MATTERS**

Understanding why your motivation has flatlined is the first step to actually addressing it. When the cause is burnout, sometimes the solution is rest and recovery. When the cause is adaptation, the solution may be novelty or meaning. When the cause is low dopamine, it may be professional help. The point is: Low motivation is information, not a personal flaw. ■

Map the Digital Temptations

Digital platforms can be great in many ways; they connect you to friends and family despite physical distance. But when it comes to your dopamine system, they are engineered to constantly release dopamine through novelty, social validation, and variable rewards so that you get hooked. And not every digital platform affects you equally. This exercise helps you identify which apps, notifications, and features are most effective at hijacking your dopamine system.

1 **List your top five digital time sinks.** These are the apps or platforms that cause you to lose track of time most easily. Examples include social media, gaming, streaming, shopping, news, or messaging.

1. ....
2. ....
3. ....
4. ....
5. ....

2 **For each time sink you've listed, identify the specific "hook."** What feature of that app or platform keeps you so engaged? Is it the not knowing of what you will come across as you scroll? Likes, comments, and other validation? Limited-time offers and price deals? Progress bars or achievement systems?

1. Hook: ....
2. Hook: ....
3. Hook: ....
4. Hook: ....
5. Hook: ....

3 **Track your time spent on each of these platforms for the next full week.**
Use the following chart:

PLATFORM	DAY 1	DAY 2	DAY 3	DAY 4	DAY 5	DAY 6	DAY 7
(e.g., Instagram)							

Add up the total time spent on digital platforms for each day:

DAY 1	DAY 2	DAY 3	DAY 4	DAY 5	DAY 6	DAY 7

Which platform did you use the most?

4 **Now, think about what made you reach for each platform.** Was it a certain time of day, like after work or when you woke up? When you felt lonely or bored? Use the following space to reflect.

WHY THIS EXERCISE **MATTERS**

Understanding exactly what platforms hijack your dopamine is the first step to reclaiming control. Once you are able to identify your own biggest time sucks and what makes you feel tempted to use them, you can start making intentional choices about what you spend time on and for how long. ■

Figure Out What Digital Compulsion Has Cost You

One of the most powerful motivators for change is recognizing what your current digital habits are costing you. This exercise makes that cost more tangible. As you move through the prompts, keep in mind that this is not about shame; it is about honest reflection, which fuels genuine commitment.

1 **Reflect on the quality of your sleep over the past month.** Have you been getting an average of eight hours each night? Do you find yourself waking up in the middle of the night, or are you struggling to fall asleep?

2 **Consider your screen use in the hours leading up to bedtime and immediately upon waking.** Do you "wind down" by scrolling through social media? Reach for your phone if you wake up at night? Check emails in bed in the morning?

3 Examine your focus and productivity over the past month. Have you been able to concentrate on work or creative tasks for long periods, or does deep or extended concentration feel challenging? Have you been getting things done swiftly, or are tasks piling up?

4 Consider how your screen use has played into your focus and productivity. Have you been able to concentrate on work or creative tasks without your phone nearby? How often did you get interrupted by notifications or urges to check your email?

5 **Assess your in-person relationships over the past month.** Have you been distracted during meals or conversations? Missed moments with loved ones? Found yourself comparing your life to others and feeling inadequate?

6 **Consider how your screen use has impacted your relationships.** Were you distracted during meals because of message notifications? Did you miss special moments because you were on your phone? Do you find yourself comparing your relationships to those seen on social media?

7 **Reflect on your mood and emotional resilience over the past month.** Have you felt unsatisfied or stressed? Avoided unpleasant feelings rather than faced them?

8 **Consider how your screen use is impacting your emotional health.** Do you reach for devices when you feel stressed, unsatisfied, bored, lonely, etc.? Do you feel worse after using these distractions?

9 **Add up the costs.** Looking at all four areas of sleep, focus, relationships, and emotions, reflect honestly on what digital compulsion has taken from you.

WHY THIS EXERCISE **MATTERS**

Making the invisible costs visible motivates change. When you can clearly see what you are sacrificing—sleep, focus, connection, peace of mind—you build real incentive to interrupt the patterns that aren't serving you. ■

CHAPTER 2

Hitting the Reset Button

As you discovered in Chapter 1, modern life is built to hijack your attention. From social feeds, to the constant ping of notifications, to the uncertain rewards you *may* receive as you swipe, technology targets your dopamine system and keeps you trapped in a state of overstimulation. This relentless noise raises your brain's threshold for satisfaction, making the experiences of real life feel flat and eventually leading to burnout. Fortunately, you can hit the reset button through a "dopamine detox": a strategic break from stimulation that lowers that threshold and helps you regain control of your attention.

In this chapter, you will use what you learned about your current dopamine patterns to design a realistic detox. You will also reinforce this detox by practicing intentional rest and considering how trauma may impact your dopamine system. These tools will help you interrupt compulsive habit patterns, not eliminate technology altogether. By deliberately reducing overstimulation, recovering before exhaustion sets in, and factoring in impactful past experiences, you'll create the conditions your nervous system needs for better balance.

Identify Where You Need a Break

Before you can plan a detox, you need more information about what is truly hijacking your dopamine system. This exercise helps you dig deeper into the specific habits that deserve a reset.

1 **Think of the digital platforms, foods, substances, shopping, games, or achievement cycles you interact with daily.** Which ones do you tend to reach for automatically and have a hard time stopping? Reflect in the space provided.

2 **Use your reflection to identify the top five habits hijacking your dopamine system:**

1.

2.

3.

4.

5.

3 **For each of these five habits, describe:** the cue (what triggers you to start that habit), the craving (how it feels in your body and mind when you are doing this habit), the immediate reward of that habit (temporary relief from boredom, feeling validated, etc.), and the long-term cost of that habit (lost sleep, reduced focus, disconnection from others, etc.).

Habit	Cue	Craving	Immediate Reward	Long-Term Cost

4 **Choose one to three habits to focus on for your detox.** Start with the habits that have the greatest mismatch between immediate reward and long-term cost.

The habit(s) I will include in my detox:

WHY THIS EXERCISE **MATTERS**

A detox is most effective when it targets specific habits that affect you personally. Naming the habits that distort your reward system is the first step in creating a realistic, focused reset you can actually follow through on. ■

Personalize Your Detox

A successful detox is intentional and time-limited, and it involves replacing bad habits rather than just quitting them. This exercise helps you build a clear, doable detox plan with the habits you identified in the previous exercise.

1 **Define your detox window.** When will you do the detox? How long will you step away from the chosen habits? Twenty-four hours? One weekend? One week? Two weeks? (It's recommended to do at least twenty-four hours, and no more than two weeks.)

Habit:

Detox start date and time:

Total duration:

Habit:

Detox start date and time:

Total duration:

---

2 **Write clear rules for each habit you're detoxing from.** What exactly is allowed and not allowed? Be specific. For example: "No social media apps at all, but texting close family is allowed," or "No online shopping; essential groceries are okay."

Habit:

Detox start date and time:

Total duration:

Habit:

Detox start date and time:

Total duration:

---

3 **Plan healthy replacements for your habits.** Identify the times of day or emotional states when you are most likely to crave your old habits. Plan specific alternative actions for those moments (e.g., walk, call a friend, read, stretch, journal, cook, breathe).

4 **Set your intention.** Why are you doing this detox? What do you hope to notice, learn, or change?

WHY THIS EXERCISE **MATTERS**

Detox without structure is hard for anyone to follow through on. When you define the amount of time, rules, and replacements, you signal to your nervous system that this is a planned break, not a punishment. That mindset is exactly what you'll need for success and meaningful insight. ■

Ride the Waves of Detoxing

During a detox, your brain will protest. Cravings, boredom, and restlessness are not signs of failure; they are evidence that your reward system is adjusting. This exercise helps you observe rather than obey those protesting signals.

1 **For each day of your detox, log your strongest urges.** Use this space to note the date, time, what triggered the urge, how intense the urge was, and what you did instead. (Depending on how long you chose to detox for, continue this log on a separate piece of paper or in a notebook.)

Date	Time	Trigger	Intensity	What I Did

2 **Notice emotional patterns.** What feelings occur most often when you cannot reach for your habit—anxiety, boredom, sadness, emptiness, or irritation? Write about what you notice in the space provided.

3 **Identify any surprising pleasures or moments of calm.** During the detox, did you notice small things feeling more vivid—food tasting better, conversations feeling richer, sleep improving, and nature feeling more soothing? Write about your experience in the following space.

WHY THIS EXERCISE **MATTERS**

Tracking cravings and emotional shifts turns discomfort into simple information. Instead of being dragged down by urges (or even self-critical of them), you become a curious observer of your own brain. This is where real learning—and real rewiring—during detox begins. ■

Build Your Post-Detox Dopamine Menu

The most important part of a dopamine detox is what happens after it ends. This exercise helps you deliberately design your life post-detox so you do not simply return to old habits.

1 **Reflect on the most significant insights from your detox.** What did you learn about your triggers, cravings, sources of satisfaction, and capacity for discomfort? Reflect in the following space.

2 **Decide what comes back, what stays out, and what changes.** For each habit you've detoxed from, choose whether to: reintroduce it with limits, replace it with a healthier alternative, or remove it entirely for now.

Habit	Reintroduce	Replace	Remove
	☐	☐	☐
	☐	☐	☐
	☐	☐	☐
	☐	☐	☐
	☐	☐	☐
	☐	☐	☐

Limits or replacements I will be enforcing:

3 **Add at least three new "menu items" you discovered during the detox.** These are activities, rituals, or connections that felt genuinely good or nourishing when you had the space to try them during your detox. Examples include a long walk without headphones, cooking a meal from scratch, an unstructured conversation with someone you trust, or journaling without a prompt.

1. ______________________________

2. ______________________________

3. ______________________________

4 **Schedule your next "mini-detox" or review.** Instead of thinking of detox as a one-time event, plan periodic resets or times when you will review how things are going and whether another detox is needed (for example, once per month or once every few months).

My next planned reset or review:

____

____

____

____

____

____

WHY THIS EXERCISE **MATTERS**

Without a post-detox plan, your brain will slip back to the easiest, fastest rewards: the habits you worked to detox from. When you consciously decide what to keep, what to change, and what to let go of, you turn a temporary reset into a long-term shift in your dopamine system. ■

Make Device-Free Zones and Rituals

Creating physical and temporal boundaries around technology is one of the most powerful tools for success both during and after a dopamine detox. This exercise helps you design your environment to support your well-being as you detox and for the long term.

1 **Choose one device-free zone in your home.** This is a space where phones, tablets, and screens are not allowed. The location might be your bedroom, dining table, or bathroom.

My device-free zone:

Why I chose this space:

2 **Design a ritual for this zone.** What activity will you anchor in this space? Examples include reading, journaling, a meal without distractions, meditation, a hobby, or family time.

The ritual I will practice in this space:

3 **Create the boundary.** How will you enforce this device-free zone? Will you leave your phone in another room? Will you use a physical barrier, such as a basket? Will you set a timer?

How I will maintain this boundary:

4 **Track your experience.** For two weeks, practice this ritual every day. Use the following space to note how it feels when you get the urge to bring devices into this space and whether you experience any shifts in calm, focus, or satisfaction over the two weeks and afterward.

WHY THIS EXERCISE **MATTERS**

Device-free zones are not about punishment; they are about protection. By physically removing that temptation, you make things easier on your willpower and give your nervous system permission to access deeper states of calm, focus, and presence. Over time, these zones can become the most restorative parts of your day. ▪

Plan for Regular Recovery Periods

The modern world praises action over rest. But when it comes to your dopamine system, periods of inaction are essential in order for your brain to reset and prepare for the next upcoming task. This exercise helps you recognize when this downtime is needed and will show you how to schedule it in.

1 **List your current recovery practices.** What do you do to rest and recharge? Examples include sleep, meditation, time in nature, creative hobbies, time with loved ones, or simple quiet time:

2 **Honestly assess your list.** Are these practices intentional or accidental? Do you rest only when you collapse from exhaustion, or do you schedule recovery as part of your routine? How much time per week do you genuinely spend in recovery?

3 **Design a recovery ritual for this week.** Choose one deliberate recovery practice you will do three times this week. This must be something low-stimulation (not scrolling or binge-watching, which are pseudo-recovery). It should feel genuinely restorative. Include information about when you will do it each day and for how long.

#1

#2

#3

4 After completing your recovery ritual, reflect on the quality of the experience. Did you notice your nervous system slowing down? When did you start to feel genuinely restored? Did the temptation to "do something" pull at you during the recovery time?

WHY THIS EXERCISE **MATTERS**

When you normalize recovery and treat these natural dips in dopamine as an essential part of life rather than a failure, you stop yourself from burning out. Your dopamine system stays responsive, your motivation remains sustainable, and genuine pleasure becomes possible again. ■

Explore How Trauma Affects Dopamine

Trauma leaves distinct fingerprints on the dopamine system and therefore requires a special approach when it comes to resetting and recovering. If you have experienced trauma in the past—perhaps through a significant loss or another painful event—this exercise will help you identify your specific dopamine pattern. (If you have not experienced trauma, you can skip this exercise.) Understanding how your brain is responding to trauma is the first step to rewiring it.

1 **Reflect on what happened following your trauma.** Did your emotional experience change? Did pleasure become harder to access? Did you find yourself reaching for relief behaviors?

2 Following a 1 to 10 scale, rate your current experience across these four areas (with 1 being minimal experience and 10 being frequent experience).

Numbness (feeling flat, disconnected, or unable to feel):

1 2 3 4 5 6 7 8 9 10

Compulsive urges (repeating behaviors to seek relief: binging on food, work, substances, or scrolling):

1 2 3 4 5 6 7 8 9 10

Anxiety (hypervigilance, worry, or difficulty relaxing):

1 2 3 4 5 6 7 8 9 10

Avoidance (withdrawing from people, activities, or difficult emotions):

1 2 3 4 5 6 7 8 9 10

3 Identify the pattern in your trauma response.

Identify the pattern in your trauma response. Using what you found in the previous steps, write about the pattern. Do you primarily go numb? Do you compulsively seek relief? Do you live in a state of anxiety? Do you isolate?

4 Reflect on how this response impacts your relationships, work, and daily life.

Reflect on how this response impacts your relationships, work, and daily life. For example, do you have trouble connecting with others on a deeper level as a result of isolating yourself?

5 **List the specific compulsions or avoidance behaviors you use to escape discomfort.** When your trauma comes to the surface, what things do you reach for to curb or avoid the uncomfortable feelings of pain, anxiety, numbness, etc.? Be honest and nonjudgmental.

WHY THIS EXERCISE **MATTERS**

Recognizing your trauma-shaped dopamine pattern is not about judgment; it is about understanding. These patterns were adaptive; they helped you survive. But now they may be keeping you stuck in a space of dopamine imbalance. By naming the patterns clearly, you move a big step closer to rewiring those patterns. ■

Disrupt Harmful Cycles

One of the most powerful ways to restore dopamine after trauma is to reclaim agency—the sense that you can make choices and direct your own life. This exercise helps you practice small, deliberate acts that interrupt old patterns and activate your brain's reward system.

1 **Choose one compulsion or avoidance behavior from the previous exercise you want to interrupt.** This should be something you engage in regularly that leaves you feeling worse afterward (not genuinely better).

The behavior I want to interrupt:

2 **Identify the triggers for this behavior.** When and why do you turn to this behavior? What emotion, time, or situation comes right before it?

3 **Plan a specific interruption.** Instead of trying to rely on willpower alone, pick a concrete action that disrupts that pattern. For example: If you compulsively scroll, keep your phone in another room. If you binge eat, go for a five-minute walk first. If you isolate, text a friend. The action should be small and doable, not overwhelming.

My interruption strategy:

4 **Track your experience for one week.** Each time you notice a trigger, practice your chosen interruption for it. Note what happens. Does the urge diminish? Do you feel more agency?

DAY 1

DAY 2

DAY 3

DAY 4

DAY 5

DAY 6

DAY 7

5 **How did it feel to reclaim the ability to choose for yourself?**

WHY THIS EXERCISE **MATTERS**

Each time you choose a new response instead of defaulting to the patterns shaped by trauma, you rewire your dopamine system toward agency, resilience, and genuine reward. Over time, these small acts add up. ■

CHAPTER 3

Setting Up Your Body, Mind, and Spaces for Balanced Dopamine

Lack of motivation is often treated as a failure of grit or discipline. Many assume that if you just try harder, push longer, or care more deeply, the problem will resolve itself. But motivation is not a moral virtue or a character flaw—it is a physical reality rooted in your dopamine system. No amount of resolve can reliably override a brain that has been depleted by chronic sleep loss, erratic nutrition, insufficient light exposure, or long stretches of physical inactivity. When your body and environment aren't used to their full potential, motivation goes offline.

This chapter invites you to shift your focus away from mental toughness and toward tangible support. Instead of asking why you can't force yourself to act, you'll learn how to assess whether your body has the raw materials it needs to make action feel possible in the first place. You'll get practical tools to examine what governs your drive—light exposure, sleep hygiene, and nutritional intake—and identify where small but consequential deficits may be sabotaging your efforts. Then, you'll redesign your environment so that it works *with* your biology rather than against it.

Work with Your Body's Natural Rhythm

Your brain's internal clock, or circadian rhythm, regulates your dopamine levels, energy, and mood. Your circadian rhythm itself is controlled by your exposure to light—daylight, along with screens and other artificial sources. This exercise will help you determine whether your light exposure is either supporting or sabotaging your dopamine system.

1 **For three days, track your exposure to light.** When did you first see sunlight? How much time did you spend outdoors? When did you start looking at screens? When did you dim the lights for the evening? Fill in your findings here:

DAY 1	DAY 2	DAY 3
Time of first sunlight:	Time of first sunlight:	Time of first sunlight:
Time outdoors:	Time outdoors:	Time outdoors:
Evening screen use:	Evening screen use:	Evening screen use:
Lights dimmed:	Lights dimmed:	Lights dimmed:
Lights turned off:	Lights turned off:	Lights turned off:

2 **For each day, note how much energy you have in the morning and how tired you feel in the evening.** Did you wake up feeling alert? Did you feel naturally sleepy at bedtime? You can write something like "very tired," or use a number scale if preferred.

DAY 1	DAY 2	DAY 3
Morning energy:	Morning energy:	Morning energy:
Evening sleepiness:	Evening sleepiness:	Evening sleepiness:

3 Identify one change you can make to improve your light exposure.

Based on what you found out in the previous steps, what is one slight adjustment you can make to have more energy in the daytime and/or get better sleep at night (e.g., a ten-minute morning walk, no screens after 9 p.m., using warmer light in the evening)?

WHY THIS EXERCISE **MATTERS**

Light is a powerful tool for regulating dopamine. Getting good light exposure—bright light in the morning and dim light at night—is like tuning your body's internal clock so that your dopamine system sends signals for energy and motivation on a naturally recurring schedule. ■

Shake Off Inertia

Movement is your brain's ancient signal for preparing to engage with your surroundings. This exercise helps you find ways to weave more movement into your day to break through lethargy and activate your dopamine system.

1 Honestly assess your current daily movement habits.

Minutes of deliberate movement:

Minutes of sitting:

2 List five forms of movement you genuinely enjoy (or used to enjoy). This is not about what you "should" do. Rather, think about activities that feel good to you (e.g., walking, dancing, stretching, gardening, hiking).

1. ______
2. ______
3. ______
4. ______
5. ______

3 **Design four "movement snacks" to break up long periods of sitting.** These should be two- to five-minute activities you can do at your desk or in your home—wherever you spend most of your time sitting (e.g., ten squats, a short walk around the block, a three-minute stretch).

Movement snack #1:

Movement snack #2:

Movement snack #3:

Movement snack #4:

4 **Schedule a more extended movement session for this week.** Choose one of your enjoyable activities from Step 2 and plan to do it at a specific date and time for at least thirty minutes. Treat it as a nonnegotiable appointment.

Activity:

Date and time:

WHY THIS EXERCISE **MATTERS**

A body in motion keeps a mind in motion. Even small bursts of movement send powerful signals to your brain, releasing dopamine and other feel-good chemicals that combat inertia and prime you for focused, motivated activity. ■

Fuel Your Brain in the Kitchen

The food you eat provides the literal building blocks for your dopamine system. This exercise helps you examine your current nutritional habits so you can make small shifts to better support your brain.

1 **For three days, track what you eat and when you eat it.** Do not judge; just observe. Note mealtimes, snacks, and any highly processed or sugary foods.

DAY 1	DAY 2	DAY 3

2 **Notice how your food choices affect your energy and focus.** After which meals or snacks do you feel stable energy? After which do you feel a crash or brain fog?

Foods that give me stable energy:

Foods that lead me to have a crash:

3 **Identify one nutritional upgrade.** What is one simple change you can make to better support your dopamine system (e.g., adding protein to breakfast, swapping a sugary snack for fruits and nuts, or eating a nourishing lunch instead of skipping it altogether)?

4 **Plan to incorporate two dopamine-building foods this week.** Tyrosine-rich foods like eggs, beans, seeds, fish, and nuts are especially beneficial to your dopamine system. Commit to including two of them into your diet this week. Write about which ones you choose and when you plan to eat them.

#1	#2

WHY THIS EXERCISE **MATTERS**

You can't build a thriving dopamine system without the foundation of nutrition. Providing your brain with the raw materials it needs through whole, nourishing foods is key to stable moods, consistent energy, and sustainable motivation. ■

Make Sleep Your Sanctuary

Sleep is when your brain cleans house and rebalances your dopamine system for the next day. This exercise helps you protect and prioritize your rest.

1 **Rate your sleep quality for the past week (with 1 being very bad sleep and 10 being great sleep).** Do you struggle to fall and/or stay asleep at night? How rested do you feel when you wake up?

Average sleep quality for this past week:

1 2 3 4 5 6 7 8 9 10

2 **Identify your greatest sleep saboteur.** When you think about your sleep for the past week, what was the one thing that consistently stood in the way of good sleep (e.g., late-night screen time, caffeine too late, inconsistent bedtime, stress/worry)?

My greatest sleep saboteur:

3 **Design a thirty-minute wind-down ritual.** This is a set routine of calming activities you will do before bed to signal to your brain it is time to rest. Crucially, this ritual must be screen-free.

4 **Commit to your new wind-down ritual for the next three nights.** Notice how it affects your ability to fall asleep and the quality of your rest. Reflect on your experience in the space provided.

WHY THIS EXERCISE MATTERS

A tired brain is an unmotivated brain. Protecting your sleep is not a luxury; it is the single most effective way to ensure your dopamine system is reset, responsive, and ready for the challenges of the next day. ■

Figure Out Where Your Space Helps or Hurts

Your environment constantly "talks" to your dopamine system. Some spaces invite focus; others pull you into distraction without you even noticing. This exercise helps you see and redesign the environments that keep your dopamine unbalanced.

1 **Choose one habit or project you want to make easier for yourself.** Examples include writing, studying, exercising, planning, or creative work.

2 Identify three ways your current environment makes this habit or project more complicated. Look at your desk, your room, your devices, and your routines. Where is there clutter? What things easily distract you or make it difficult for you to stay motivated?

1. ______________________________

____

____

2. ______________________________

____

____

3. ______________________________

____

____

3 Identify what in your current environment helps you focus on this habit or project. Are there any cues that support this habit/project (e.g., an organized desk, a favorite chair, a nearby park, a quiet time of day)?

____

____

____

____

____

____

____

____

4 **Choose three environment changes to make.** These changes should reduce the challenges of focusing on the habit/project and increase cues that help.

CHANGE #1	CHANGE #2	CHANGE #3
Make it easier to start:	Remove or relocate a distraction:	Add a visual or physical cue that invites the habit:

WHY THIS EXERCISE **MATTERS**

Dopamine responds strongly to cues. When you shape your environment so that the helpful cues are apparent, and the unhelpful ones are harder to reach, motivation starts to feel less like a fight and more like a natural next step. ■

Train Your Brain to Switch "On"

In addition to a motivating environment, you can also deliberately signal to your brain that it's time to get going by repeating a specific ritual before you get started with an activity. The ritual tells your brain, "Now we begin." Over time, it becomes linked to focus and forward movement.

1 **Pick one activity that requires focused effort.** My chosen activity:

2 **Create a three-step ritual you will do every time before starting this activity.** Keep it simple and sensory. Examples include brewing tea, opening a specific document, playing a certain playlist, stretching, setting a twenty-five-minute timer, or putting your phone in another room.

STEP #1	STEP #2	STEP #3

3 **Test your ritual five times.** Each time, do the ritual before starting the activity. Afterward, briefly note how easy or hard it was to begin the activity (use the following spaces).

#1

#2

#3

#4

#5

WHY THIS EXERCISE **MATTERS**

You can train your own brain. When it learns that certain sensory cues are followed by meaningful progress, it begins to release dopamine in anticipation, making it easier to overcome inertia and get right into the work. ■

Use Your "Off" Switch

> Motivation cannot be sustained without recovery. If you solely focus on priming your dopamine system for effort without considering how to end that effort, your system is likely to experience burnout.

1 **Describe how you currently end your workday or other intense effort.** Do you have a clear stopping point, or do you "half-work" into the evening?

2 **Create a simple shutdown ritual that marks the end of the workday/effort.** Examples include closing and putting away your laptop, writing tomorrow's top three tasks, turning off notifications, changing clothes, or stepping outside.

3 Use this shutdown ritual for the next three days and notice what changes each day. Do you sleep better? Ruminate less? Are you ready to start the next day?

WHY THIS EXERCISE **MATTERS**

Recovery is not wasted time; it is dopamine maintenance. When your brain trusts that effort will be followed by genuine rest, it becomes easier to fully commit during work periods because it no longer has to brace for endless strain. ■

Embrace Comfort Rituals

Dopamine does not function well when your nervous system is stressed or feels threatened. When your body is in a survival state following trauma, dopamine is redirected toward hypervigilance rather than motivation and reward. Comfort rituals signal to your nervous system, "This is a moment where I am safe and cared for," so your dopamine system can better work for you. This exercise will help you create personalized rituals that help your brain feel more relaxed and safe after trauma. If this exercise doesn't feel relevant to you, you can skip it.

1 **Identify one time of day when you could make room for a small, nourishing ritual.** This can be in the morning, midday, or evening—whatever feels realistic.

2 Design a five- to ten-minute ritual that engages at least two senses. This might include warm tea, soft music, gentle movement, a favorite blanket, or sitting in natural light. Write down the ritual and which senses it engages here:

3 **Practice this ritual every day for the next seven days.** Consistency is key. Your brain needs repetition to learn: "This pattern equals safety." After three days, how is it feeling? After seven days, what has shifted?

4 Reflect on what this ritual is teaching your nervous system. What does it mean when you do this ritual? What is the signal? (For example, it might signal: I am safe. I am cared for. I am allowed to slow down. This moment belongs to me.)

What my ritual signals:

WHY THIS EXERCISE **MATTERS**

Trauma fragments your body's sense of safety and disrupts your dopamine system's balance. A daily comfort ritual is like an anchor, reminding your body and dopamine system that safety and nourishment are real and available. Repetition is rewiring. ■

CHAPTER 4

Building Your Own Dopamine Menu

You've figured out where there is imbalance, hit the reset button, and started working with your body and surroundings. Now, it's time to create a long-term plan for maintaining a balanced dopamine system. A Dopamine Menu is a highly personalized collection of activities, habits, and rituals that match your brain's needs. It is made up of main courses, side dishes, and desserts. Main courses are staple activities that deliver deep engagement (such as focused projects, immersive learning, or creative expression) and recharge your reward system. Side dishes are short bursts of novelty, movement, or brief social connection (such as a quick call with a friend or a ten-minute walk) that complement your main courses. Desserts are restorative activities for mental and emotional renewal, including sleep and mindful relaxation. A special combination of all three can replace the steady stream of "junk dopamine" (the "empty calories" of doom scrolling, impulsive snacking, and constant novelty) and bring true satisfaction.

In this chapter, you will examine your current Dopamine Menu, personalize it, and fine-tune menu items as needed. You will also make time to recognize and celebrate triumphs as they come, and notice what it feels like when you are content.

Redefine Reward

In a world full of instant gratification, it is easy to confuse stimulation with meaningful reward. This exercise helps you distinguish between short-lived highs and experiences that create a more profound sense of joy and purpose. This ability to differentiate genuine reward from a quick hit will be the foundation for building your Dopamine Menu and filling it with those real rewards.

1 In the past week, recall three quick-hit pleasures you reached for. These can be scrolling, snacking, online shopping, binge-watching, impulse multitasking—anything that gives you an instant boost of dopamine. For each one, write how you felt right before engaging in them and how you felt ten minutes after.

Quick-Hit Pleasure #1	Quick-Hit Pleasure #2	Quick-Hit Pleasure #3

2 **Recall three quiet satisfactions from the past week.** These might include finishing a task, having a real conversation, moving your body, helping someone, or making progress on a long-term goal—anything that left you feeling content afterward. For each one, write how you felt right before starting that activity and how you felt later that day.

Quiet Satisfaction #1	Quiet Satisfaction #2	Quiet Satisfaction #3

3 **Reflect on the difference.** What do your quick-hit rewards and your quiet satisfactions have in common? How do they differ in terms of your energy and mood, and what they mean to you?

4 **Choose one quiet satisfaction you would like to enjoy more often.** Examples include finishing a book, completing a home project, having a long, uninterrupted conversation, or cooking a meal and sitting down to eat it without screens.

5 **Write down one small way you could make this quiet satisfaction easier to start in the coming week.** Examples include laying out your walking shoes, scheduling a fifteen-minute focus block, or texting a friend to check in.

WHY THIS EXERCISE **MATTERS**

Dopamine is not just about chasing pleasure. It is about what you teach your brain to value. By choosing deeper satisfactions over quick hits, you start to rewire your reward system to choose more meaningful acts. Your brain begins to recognize effort, connection, and progress as powerful sources of reward. Over time, this shifts your motivation away from constantly chasing cravings and toward a more stable, deeper sense of joy. ▪

Savor the Win

The most forgotten act in the race for dopamine highs is celebration. Caught in the endless chase, people often rush past their wins to get to the next one, and the next. This exercise helps you take a pause to celebrate your hard work. This, in turn, trains your brain to register and retain reward from the activities that you will be putting on your Dopamine Menu.

1 **Recall a smaller win from this week that you glossed over.** Did you send a difficult email? Did you stick to a healthy choice? Did you complete a quick chore you were avoiding?

2 **Replay the tape.** Close your eyes and mentally relive the moment you identified in Step 1 for thirty seconds. Do not focus on what you have to do next. Focus entirely on the fact that it is done. Then, write down one specific detail about why this win was beneficial for you or how it made your life slightly better.

3 **Design a ritual for your next achievement.** Decide how you will mark the completion of your next task. This must be an action, not just a thought. Examples include playing a specific victory song, taking a five-minute walk outside, ringing a bell, high-fiving a partner, or verbally saying, "I am finished."

The task I will complete:	**The ritual I will perform:**

4 **Check in after the ritual.** After you perform this ritual, note how you felt. Did you feel more satisfied with this win than you usually do after finishing something?

WHY THIS EXERCISE **MATTERS**

Savoring the win does not come naturally to many, especially if your dopamine system is imbalanced; it must be practiced. By creating a ritualized pause after an achievement, you force your brain to acknowledge the reward. This prevents burnout and trains your dopamine system for deeper satisfaction. ■

Swap Engineered Rewards with Real Ones

Your brain does not function solely through deprivation. To break digital compulsion, you need to replace engineered dopamine hits (those created by someone to be extremely compelling and require little effort from you, e.g., push notifications) with authentic ones. You will use what you uncover in this exercise to help fill your Dopamine Menu with truly rewarding activities.

1. **List the activities you used to enjoy that do *not* involve screens.** Think of hobbies, creative pursuits, time in nature, physical activity, face-to-face connection, or quiet practices.

2. **For each activity you listed in Step 1, write down why you have not been doing it lately.** Did you forget about it? Did it seem less appealing than screens? Did you convince yourself you did not have the time? Be honest.

3 Choose one activity to swap. Identify one digital platform you will reduce (not eliminate) and one offline activity you will swap it with. For example, instead of scrolling through Instagram for thirty minutes after work, you will take a walk or read a chapter of a book.

Platform I will reduce my time on:

Current time spent on platform:

Reduced time I will be on platform:

Activity I will swap it with:

When I will do this swap:

Notes:

4 **Commit to this swap for fourteen days.** Track how you feel during this time. Do you miss the digital platform? Does the offline activity activate dopamine differently? Do you sleep better? Focus better? Feel calmer or more connected?

WHY THIS EXERCISE **MATTERS**

When you replace an engineered dopamine hit with an authentic one, your dopamine system starts to shift its sense of reward. Over time, you train your brain to recognize that real satisfaction comes from presence, connection, and meaningful activity—not from digital algorithms designed to keep you hooked. ■

Dig Deeper Into Your Current Dopamine Menu

Before you can build a better Dopamine Menu, you need to clearly see what your current one looks like. This exercise helps you track your activities and notice which ones genuinely nourish your dopamine system and which ones are just "junk food" that leave you depleted.

1 **For five days, record every significant activity, interaction, and experience.** Include work tasks, movement, food, social time, hobbies, screen time, and rest. Note the time spent on each.

DAY 1

DAY 2

DAY 3

DAY 4

DAY 5

2 **For each activity you recorded, go back and rate how much engagement it created, how much it satisfied you afterward, and how much energy it left you with.** (Use a rating scale of 1 to 10, with 1 being low engagement/satisfaction/energy and 10 being high engagement/satisfaction/energy.) Write your rating next to the activity in the chart.

3 **Categorize your activities.** Based on what you learned previously about the Dopamine Menu, which activities are main courses (deep engagement, meaningful work, and absolute satisfaction)? Which are side dishes (brief novelty, social connection, quick energy boosts)? Which are desserts (truly calming and renewing)? Which are junk foods (leave you depleted, numb, or restless)?

Main courses:

Desserts:

Side dishes:

Junk foods:

4 **Reflect on the balance between courses.** Are you getting enough deep engagement? Enough restoration? Too much junk food? Is your current menu serving your actual needs?

WHY THIS EXERCISE **MATTERS**

It's easy to go through the day on autopilot, unaware of which activities are actually nourishing your dopamine system and which are depleting it. By looking closer at your current Dopamine Menu, you are taking the first step toward creating one that works for you. ■

Build Your Ideal Dopamine Menu

Now that you see your current patterns, you can build your ideal Dopamine Menu. This exercise helps you identify the activities and practices that should be central to your life.

1 **List the top five activities that create deep engagement and satisfaction for you.** These activities will be your menu's main courses; they should keep you fully engaged, make you lose track of time, and leave you feeling genuinely fulfilled. Examples include creative projects, focused work, meaningful conversations, physical pursuits, learning, or helping others:

1. ....
2. ....
3. ....
4. ....
5. ....

2 **List the top five practices that add novelty, lightness, and connection to your day.** These are quick hits that prevent boredom and add flavor to everyday life—the things that will be your menu's side dishes. Examples include a short walk, a funny conversation, trying something new, a small win, time with a friend, or brief learning (e.g., researching something online that you've been curious about):

1. ______________________________

2. ______________________________

3. ______________________________

4. ______________________________

5. ______________________________

3 **List the top five practices that genuinely calm and renew you.** These are your menu's desserts; they should leave you feeling restored, not distracted. Examples include meditation, time in nature, specific music, journaling, warm baths, quiet time, or creative hobbies done slowly:

1. ______________________________

2. ______________________________

3. ______________________________

4. ______________________________

5. ______________________________

4 **Design your ideal weekly menu.** How many times per week would you like to enjoy each main course? How often would you like to enjoy the side dishes? How much time do you want to leave for restorative desserts? Write out a realistic, ideal week. Aim for one or two main courses, two or three side dishes, and one restorative dessert every day.

Monday's Menu		
Main Courses:	Side Dishes:	Dessert:

Tuesday's Menu		
Main Courses:	Side Dishes:	Dessert:

Wednesday's Menu		
Main Courses:	Side Dishes:	Dessert:

Thursday's Menu		
Main Courses:	Side Dishes:	Dessert:

Friday's Menu		
Main Courses:	Side Dishes:	Dessert:

Saturday's Menu		
Main Courses:	Side Dishes:	Dessert:

Sunday's Menu		
Main Courses:	Side Dishes:	Dessert:

WHY THIS EXERCISE **MATTERS**

This is about intentionality. When you consciously design your ideal menu, you stop being a passive participant in your own dopamine system. You become the chef, deliberately choosing what nourishes you. ■

Test Your New Dopamine Menu

You can't know if your ideal menu actually works until you try it. Through this exercise, you'll live your new menu for two weeks and track what happens.

1 **For two weeks, commit to following your designed Dopamine Menu as closely as possible.** This does not have to be perfect; life happens. But do your best to include your main courses, side dishes, and restorative desserts as planned.

2 **Each evening, rate your day from 1 to 10.** With 1 being not satisfying at all and 10 being very satisfying, how was your day? How engaged did you feel in the day's activities? Compared to a typical evening, how do you feel? More settled or more depleted? More satisfied or more restless?

	DAY	SCORE		DAY	SCORE
WEEK #1	Day 1		WEEK #2	Day 1	
	Day 2			Day 2	
	Day 3			Day 3	
	Day 4			Day 4	
	Day 5			Day 5	
	Day 6			Day 6	
	Day 7			Day 7	

3 **Track which menu items were the most satisfying.** Which main courses were the most nourishing? Which side dishes felt most energizing? Which desserts delivered the most renewal?

Most nourishing main courses:

Most energizing side dishes:

Most restorative desserts:

4 **Reflect on what needs to change.** Did some menu items not work as expected? Did you discover new menu items worth adding?

WHY THIS EXERCISE **MATTERS**

In testing out your menu, you are discovering, through real experience, what actually nourishes your specific dopamine system. These two weeks of trying things out and recording what you find can teach you quite a bit about what works best for you. ■

Fine-Tune Your Dopamine Menu

A Dopamine Menu that never changes becomes stale. The menu options stop feeling engaging or satisfying and instead become boring. This exercise helps you build the habit of regularly fine-tuning your menu so that it stays alive and responsive to your evolving needs.

1 **Schedule monthly check-ins with your menu.** On the same date each month (for example, the first Sunday), take thirty minutes to assess your menu: What is working? What has stopped feeling satisfying? What needs to be added? Use this space to start keeping track of what you discover during your check-ins:

MONTH	DATE	NOTES
Month 1		
Month 2		
Month 3		
Month 4		
Month 5		
Month 6		
Month 7		
Month 8		
Month 9		
Month 10		
Month 11		
Month 12		

2 Identify new menu items to try each season. Winter might call for different nourishment than summer. It may mean inward activities like reading or deeper conversations. Summer might be the time for more novelty and outdoor activities. Fall and spring may require a mix of novel and meditative activities. Adding seasonal specials to your menu will help it stay fresh and fulfilling throughout the year. Reflect on what items might be beneficial for each season here:

Spring specials:

Fall specials:

Summer specials:

Winter specials:

3 Watch for warning signs of imbalance. Create a simple checklist of signs that your menu needs adjustment. Examples include persistent boredom, restlessness, fatigue, irritability, loss of satisfaction, or feeling numb despite having "good" things in your schedule.

Warning Signs That My Menu Is Out of Balance
☐
☐
☐
☐
☐
☐
☐
☐
☐
☐
☐
☐
☐
☐
☐
☐
☐

4 **Commit to rotating in new items.** When one of your warning signs appears, that is your signal to refresh your menu. Add a new main course, experiment with different side dishes, or introduce a novel restorative dessert. Check your seasonal specials for ideas. Use this space to plan ahead for when one or more warning signs pop up in the future:

New Main Courses	New Side Dish Courses	New Dessert Courses

WHY THIS EXERCISE **MATTERS**

A Dopamine Menu is made to change with your own ever-changing life; it is a living system that evolves *with* you. By scheduling a regular check-in and planning for new items, you can prevent burnout, maintain engagement, and ensure that your menu continues to nourish you as your needs and preferences change. This is how motivation becomes truly sustainable. ■

Stress-Test Your Dopamine Menu

One final piece of trying out and adapting your menu is to test it out when things get more intense and you are more apt to get sidetracked. In this exercise, you will do just that.

1 **Take your menu into a high-pressure week.** Track which items you actually reach for under stress versus which ones you abandon.

2 **Reflect on what this has revealed about what your nervous system truly needs versus what you think it needs.**

WHY THIS EXERCISE **MATTERS**

A personalized Dopamine Menu is not a rigid protocol; it is a living, breathing guide that evolves with you and whatever comes your way in life. It is important to build a menu that feels doable and motivating even when stress tries to derail your efforts. This is how you and your dopamine system will flourish in the long term. ■

Practice Joy

Trauma often dulls the capacity for pleasure. You may find it hard to enjoy activities, even ones that used to bring you joy. If trauma has shifted your dopamine system, your Dopamine Menu will need a specialized step that accounts for that shift. This exercise is that step: rebuilding the baseline capacity for pleasure, so the main courses, side dishes, and desserts you have just designed can actually land as rewarding.

1 **List five activities or experiences that brought you genuine joy before trauma (or that occasionally bring you joy now).** These can be simple: a specific food, a type of music, time in nature, a hobby, or time with one particular person.

1. ____________________

2. ____________________

3. ____________________

4. ____________________

5. ____________________

2 **Choose one activity to practice this week.** Commit to engaging in it for at least fifteen to twenty minutes a couple of days this week. The goal is not to force joy but to notice if even small moments of pleasure emerge.

Activity I will practice:

____

____

____

When and how I will do it:

____

____

____

3 **While engaging, practice deliberate savoring.** Pay attention to sensory details: textures, tastes, sounds, and smells. Notice your body. Do not rush. If numbness is intense, just notice that too—without judgment. The practice is in the present, not in forcing happiness.

Day 1 observations (sensory details, feelings, any glimpses of pleasure):

Day 2 observations (sensory details, feelings, any glimpses of pleasure):

Day 3 observations (sensory details, feelings, any glimpses of pleasure):

4 **Reflect on what you discovered.** Did any pleasure emerge, even if it was small? Did presence itself feel restoring? Did the numbness shift even slightly?

What I learned about my capacity for pleasure:

WHY THIS EXERCISE **MATTERS**

Pleasure is not frivolous after trauma; it is medicine. Each time you deliberately engage in a pleasurable activity and notice even small moments of joy, you send a powerful signal to your dopamine system: Safety and reward are possible again. Over time, these moments multiply and deepen, rewiring the brain away from survival mode and toward genuine engagement with life. ■

Catch Surprise Moments of Relief

When something turns out better than expected, it is a huge boost to your dopamine system. Adding activities or experiences that you originally did not expect to be rewarding to your Dopamine Menu is a great way to evolve it. This exercise helps you notice these moments so you can work them into your living, evolving Dopamine Menu—and enjoy them when they happen.

1 **For the next week, watch for moments when something turned out better than expected.** These can be tiny: a shorter line, a kind word, or less pain than anticipated.

Moment #1	Moment #2	Moment #3
Description:	Description:	Description:
How much better than I expected:	How much better than I expected:	How much better than I expected:

2 For each moment, pause and deliberately notice it for at least thirty seconds. Do not rush past it. Let your brain register: "That was good. That was not what I expected. The world surprised me—positively."

How it felt to pause and notice:

3 Write down or say aloud one thing you are grateful for, no matter how small. Gratitude amplifies dopamine signaling.

One small thing I am grateful for:

WHY THIS EXERCISE **MATTERS**

Trauma trains the brain to scan for threats. By deliberately catching good surprises, you are slowly retraining it to notice both danger and safety. Over time, your default becomes more balanced. ■

CHAPTER 5

Finding Focus, Flow, and Creativity

You have diagnosed your patterns, reset your system, built your biological foundation, and constructed your Dopamine Menu. Now it is time to put that renewed system to work. Dopamine is not just about feeling good. It is the engine behind focus, flow, and creativity. When your reward system is calibrated correctly, deep work becomes easier, distractions lose their pull, and ideas arrive with less difficulty.

The exercises in this chapter will help you channel your recalibrated dopamine system into the work and creative pursuits that matter most to you. You'll determine what time of day your brain works best, get into a flow state of deep work, intentionally start and stop work at your own chosen times, and more. Better focus, meaningful work, and creativity are in your reach—thanks to your dopamine system.

Track Where Your Attention Actually Goes

Before you can reclaim focus, you need to clearly see where it is naturally turning. This exercise maps the invisible forces that are stealing your attention.

1 **Track your interruptions for one full workday.** Every time your attention is pulled away—by a notification, a message, an urgent request, or your own impulse to check something—note the time and what interrupted your focus.

Time	What Pulled Me

2 **Categorize the cause of each interruption.** Was it external (a colleague, a meeting, a notification)? Or was it internal (you choosing to check your email, straying from your task, or simply being curious)?

External	Internal

3 **Estimate the total time you remained focused that day.** How many minutes or hours did you have of uninterrupted work on each meaningful task?

4 **Identify your three biggest "focus killers."** Which interruptions happened most often and felt the most derailing to your focus?

#1

#2

#3

WHY THIS EXERCISE **MATTERS**

You can't fix what you can't see. Noting each distraction helps you let go of the blame you place on yourself for a lack of willpower and take back control from the distracting world you are working in. This is the first step to reclaiming your focus. ■

Determine When Your Brain Works Best

Not all times of the day are equal. Your brain has natural peaks and valleys of attention, energy, and creativity. This exercise helps you identify and protect your best work hours.

1 **For the next week, note when you naturally feel most alert and focused.** Don't force it; just observe when your mind feels clearest.

DAY 1	DAY 2	DAY 3	DAY 4	DAY 5	DAY 6	DAY 7

2 **Note when you typically feel a dip in your energy or feel scattered.** When during the day does your attention become harder to sustain?

DAY 1	DAY 2	DAY 3	DAY 4	DAY 5	DAY 6	DAY 7

3 **Identify one "golden hour" time for this week.** Based on what you discovered about your natural energy peaks and dips, schedule a sixty- to ninety-minute period when you will do your most important, meaningful work.

My golden hour:	The important work I will do:
Date: Time:	

4 **Eliminate all possible interruptions during this time.** Some ideas include silencing notifications, closing email and chat windows, putting your phone away, letting people know you are unavailable, or removing anything that might lead to distractions.

How I will protect this time:

WHY THIS EXERCISE **MATTERS**

Your dopamine system is most responsive when you align tasks with your natural rhythms of energy and focus. By scheduling just one golden hour each week, you reclaim the capacity for the kind of deep focus that makes work feel meaningful rather than scattered. ■

Get Into the Flow State

The "flow state" is when you are so absorbed in a task that time and everything else fade in the background and working on that task feels effortless. This flow happens when challenge and skill are balanced. This exercise helps you deliberately create the conditions that invite a flow state.

1 **Describe the last time you experienced a flow state at work.** When were you so engaged that time seemed to disappear and work felt effortless?

2 **Identify what made that state of flow possible.** What was different about the environment, the task, your energy, or your focus?

3 **Pick one thing you can replicate this week.** Based on your previous flow experience, what is one condition you can intentionally recreate (e.g., a quiet environment, a specific time of day, a clear objective, a sense of manageable challenge)?

4 **After you experience a flow state again, reflect on everything that made it possible.** What helped you slip into that deep engagement? These will be the things you'll want to continuously turn to whenever you want to get back into a flow state.

WHY THIS EXERCISE **MATTERS**

Flow is not random; it results from specific conditions that align with your nervous system's needs. When you understand what invites you into a flow state, you stop waiting for inspiration and start creating the circumstances where your best work happens naturally. ■

Start and Stop Work Intentionally

The brain responds powerfully to consistent cues. This exercise helps you create rituals that signal the beginning and end of a work task, so your dopamine system knows when to engage and when to shift gears or rest, giving you and your brain time to recover.

1. **Design a three- to five-minute ritual for starting work.** This will happen right before your focused work block. It should include one or more of these sensory cues: movement, sound, a specific place, a brief intention, or a grounding practice.

My starting ritual:

2. **Design a three- to five-minute ritual for ending work.** This will happen when your work block ends. It marks that ending and signals to your brain that it is time to shift gears. Examples include writing down one thing accomplished, deliberately closing the laptop, moving your body, or expressing gratitude.

My closing ritual:

3 **Practice both rituals for the next five workdays.** Commit to doing them consistently, even if they feel awkward at first. Write about how these rituals looked and what work you started and stopped.

4 **Reflect on the shift.** Did the starting ritual help you settle into focus faster? Did the closing ritual help you actually disengage from the work? How did things change over the course of the five days as you kept at it?

WHY THIS EXERCISE **MATTERS**

Rituals create internal shortcuts for certain habits you want to keep up. When your brain learns that specific cues always come before focused work (or mark that the work is done), it begins to automate the transitions into and out of that focused work—making it easier to engage deeply, change gears when ready, and rest when it's time. ■

Explore the Other Side of Novelty

It can be easy to mistake constantly engaging with novel activities (scrolling through social media, binge-watching TV) for creating something new. This exercise helps you distinguish between the two and find your balance.

1 **Track novelty for the next three days.** List the primary sources of new information or stimulation you consume (social media, news, podcasts, shows) during these days:

DAY 1	DAY 2	DAY 3

2 **Track your creativity for the same three days.** List the things you actually made, solved, wrote, or built during these days:

DAY 1	DAY 2	DAY 3

3 **Compare the two lists.** Is your dopamine system getting its "fix" mostly from passive consumption of novelty, or through real creativity?

4 **Choose one source of passive novelty to eliminate for twenty-four hours.** See if it increases your drive to create.

The novelty I will eliminate:

How my creativity was impacted (or not) by eliminating this novelty:

WHY THIS EXERCISE **MATTERS**

Passive consumption satisfies your brain's craving for novelty without requiring any effort. This can dull your drive to create. By limiting passive novelties, you leave a space in your dopamine system that your brain will naturally want to fill with active creativity. ■

Step Into Uncertainty

Dopamine spikes when you don't know what is going to happen. If your work or personal experiences feel stale, it might be because you are not taking enough creative risks that lean into uncertainty, which can lead to great rewards. This exercise helps you introduce "safe uncertainty" to your life. Safe uncertainty is a situation where the outcome is unknown but the stakes are manageable. It triggers dopamine through novelty and possibility without activating your threat system.

1 **Identify one area of your work or personal life that feels safe but also boring.** In what aspect of your work or personal life do you operate without thinking?

2 **Design a small risk.** What could you try that has an uncertain outcome (e.g., pitching a new idea, trying a new medium such as a voice memo rather than an email, sharing early work, changing your routine)?

3. **Predict the worst-case and best-case scenarios.** What are you afraid will happen? What is the potential reward?

4. **Take the risk.** After you do it, note how it felt. Did you feel more alert or driven?

WHY THIS EXERCISE **MATTERS**

Safe risks are like espresso shots for the creative part of your brain. They wake up your dopamine system and remind you that you are capable of handling the unknown. This builds creative confidence and combats stagnation. ■

Design Creative Rituals

You can train your brain to enter a creative state on command using sensory cues. When you consistently pair a ritual (e.g., lighting a candle, putting on specific music, or clearing your desk) with creative work, your brain begins releasing dopamine in anticipation of that work. This exercise helps you build a ritual that signals, "It's time to innovate."

1 **Choose a creative task you do often.** Examples include writing, coding, designing, or problem-solving.

2 **Select three sensory cues to pair with this task.** Think about sound (a specific playlist), smell (a candle), taste (coffee), touch (a specific chair), and sight (lighting).

Sensory Cue #1	Sensory Cue #2	Sensory Cue #3

3 **Pick a physical movement that will mark the start.** Examples include putting on headphones, clearing the desk, or closing your eyes for ten seconds.

4 **Test your ritual.** Use this ritual for the next three creative sessions. Does it help you settle in faster? What do you notice?

WHY THIS EXERCISE **MATTERS**

Creativity often just needs something to invite it in, and a creative ritual acts as a trigger for your brain, signaling the start. It helps you skip the procrastination phase and get straight to the task. ■

Finish Something

Dopamine is released when you are anticipating something and peaks during the pursuit, rather than when you've reached that goal. This means it can feel easy to start a project but not so easy to finish it. This exercise helps you hack your dopamine system to reward finishing a chosen task, not just starting it.

1 **List three projects or ideas you have started but not finished:**

Project #1	Project #2	Project #3

2 **Choose one to finish this week.** Pick something small enough to actually finish.

The project I will finish:

3 **Plan a celebration for when you finish.** Hacking your dopamine system to reward finishing tasks rather than just starting them calls for positive reinforcement—like a celebration. How will you mark the moment the chosen project is done (share it, print it, delete the file, buy a treat, take a walk)?

My celebration:

4 **Pay attention to the feeling of being done.** When you finish, pause and let yourself feel the satisfaction. Do not rush to the next thing. Savor the closure.

How it felt to finish:

WHY THIS EXERCISE **MATTERS**

If you only reward starting something, you will end up with a million great ideas and no finished work. By deliberately celebrating completion, you train your dopamine system to crave the finish line as much as the starting gun. ■

Prove What's Possible

It's easier to focus and be creative when you believe change is possible. But trauma and long-term stress can train your brain to expect that nothing will work, making it harder to even get started. This exercise helps break that cycle by giving you one small win—reminding your brain that effort and new experiences can still pay off. It will set you up for the focus and flow exercises that come next.

1 **Choose one tiny, low-risk change you can make this week.** This should feel manageable, not scary. Examples include taking a different route on a walk, trying a new tea, listening to a song you haven't heard in years, or rearranging one room.

My micro-change:

2 **Before you do it, predict how you will feel.** What emotion(s) or sensation(s) do you expect?

My prediction:

3 **Make the micro-change and observe what actually happens.** Did anything surprise you, even slightly? Did you feel any unexpected sensation—calmness, curiosity, or mild pleasure?

What actually happened:

4 **Repeat this with two different micro-changes this week.** Each novel experience, no matter how small, is a step toward embracing new things.

Change #2:

What I noticed:

Change #3:

What I noticed:

WHY THIS EXERCISE **MATTERS**

Trauma teaches your brain to expect danger. But micro-changes like the ones you practiced in this exercise are proof that newness can be safe. Each one activates your dopamine system, slowly shifting it toward a sustained hope. ■

Notice Moments of Forward Movement

The courage to start and share your work—despite the risk of a mistake or detour—becomes more accessible when you approach discomfort rather than avoid it. This exercise helps you see your own courage in even the smallest creative and professional risks.

1. **For the next week, notice each time you approached something uncomfortable instead of avoiding it.** This might be answering a difficult question, reaching out to someone, revisiting a painful memory with support, or even just sitting with a hard feeling instead of numbing it. Note what you approached and how you felt before and after the experience:

2. **For each instance, give yourself credit.** You had the courage to take action rather than running the other way. Write about what you want to acknowledge about your courage in each of the moments you noted in Step 1:

3 **Notice if/how your brain's predictions are starting to shift.** After approaching uncomfortable things, is it becoming less scary to keep doing so? More manageable? Record your observations here:

WHY THIS EXERCISE **MATTERS**

Dopamine reinforces what you practice. Each time you approach instead of avoid even the slightest discomforts, your brain registers: "I can handle this. I am capable. The world is not as dangerous as I thought." This is how trauma is rewired in your dopamine system. ■

CHAPTER 6

Inviting Connection, Resilience, and Deeper Meaning

Dopamine does not operate in a vacuum; it thrives on connection. While many might associate it with personal achievement and the thrill of the chase, your brain is actually hardwired to release strong reward signals through social bonding, trust, and shared purpose. Lasting fulfillment involves rooting your motivation in something far more durable than fleeting pleasures: community; deeper meaning; and the ability to risk vulnerability, misunderstanding, and everything else that comes with putting yourself out there.

Now that you have looked within to better understand your own dopamine system, it's time to explore the larger picture of other people and life's deeper meanings. An important part of the journey to making dopamine work for you, this chapter will help you map your support systems and use rituals of belonging to anchor satisfaction. You will work through loneliness, get vulnerable, choose what truly matters, and more. By actively aligning your dopamine system with connection and meaning, you ensure that your motivation is not just a quick spark that burns out when things get hard, but an enduring flame that lights your way forward.

Map Feelings of Loneliness

Not all social interaction is equally nourishing for your dopamine system. This exercise helps you distinguish between the quantity of connection (how many people you interact with) and the quality of those interactions (how deeply known and accepted you feel).

1 **List your current sources of social interaction.** Include family, close friends, colleagues, acquaintances, online communities, and group activities. For each, list how you connect (in-person, phone, text, social media, video call), and how often:

1. ....
2. ....
3. ....
4. ....
5. ....
6. ....
7. ....
8. ....
9. ....
10. ....

2 **Using a scale of 1 to 10, rate the depth of each connection you listed.** With 1 being not deeply at all and 10 being very deeply, how deeply known do you feel in each connection? Can you be vulnerable? Do they understand your struggles, not just your highlights? Use these questions to help determine your ratings.

1. ______
2. ______
3. ______
4. ______
5. ______
6. ______
7. ______
8. ______
9. ______
10. ______

3 **Using a scale of 1 to 10, reflect on how much of your social time is dedicated to surface relationships versus deep relationships.** With 1 being entirely surface level, 6 being neutral, and 10 being a strongly deep relationship, evaluate what you uncovered in the previous steps:

______

______

______

______

______

4 **Consider the mismatch.** Do you feel lonely despite having many social interactions? What is missing? Is it honesty? Vulnerability? Physical proximity? Write about what genuine belonging would look like for you.

WHY THIS EXERCISE **MATTERS**

Loneliness is not solved by gaining more and more connections; it is solved by deepening meaningful ones. This exercise helps you see clearly where your time and energy are going and whether they are nourishing the belonging you actually need or just feeding the desire for recognition. ■

Experiment with Recognition versus Resonance

Digital platforms deliver recognition—likes, comments, and visibility. Genuine relationships deliver resonance—that feeling of being understood, accepted, and emotionally seen. This exercise helps you really feel the difference, so you can focus on what is truly fulfilling.

1 **Choose one person with whom you have a surface-level digital relationship** (lots of messaging or social media interaction, but limited depth).

Name:

2 **Initiate a typical conversation with this person.** After the interaction, write about what you noticed. Was there genuine engagement or was it performative? Did you feel more connected or more drained afterward?

3 **Now identify one person in your life with whom you experience genuine resonance.** This is someone who deeply understands and accepts you. Reflect on these feelings and your connection with this person.

Name:

How I feel about them and our connection:

4 Commit to spending more intentional time with this "resonance" person. Plan a specific hangout where you are both fully present (no phones, no distractions). Afterward, reflect on how different it felt compared to other, more surface-level interactions you've recently had.

Planned activity (date and time):

After the experience, how did I feel compared to typical digital interactions?

WHY THIS EXERCISE MATTERS

Resonance activates your dopamine system on a deeper level. When you deliberately practice deeper engagement with people, you train your brain to recognize and seek genuine connection instead of settling for fleeting sparks of digital recognition. ■

Go Device-Free

One of the simplest yet most powerful ways to activate your dopamine system is to be fully present with another person. This exercise will help you create a structured practice for doing just that.

1 Identify one daily mealtime or activity where you could eliminate devices. This can occur during breakfast, dinner, a walk, or a time with a specific person or group.

The mealtime or activity:

Who I will do this with:

When it will happen:

2 **Create a clear boundary.** Consider placing your phone in another room, turning it off, or placing it in a basket. How will you signal to yourself and others that this time is sacred and undistracted?

3 Practice this for one week. Each day, engage fully without screens during your chosen time and activity. Write about each experience: What becomes possible when you are not divided between the person and the phone? What do you learn about each other? How do you feel?

4 **Reflect on the shift.** At the end of the week, dig deeper into how things went and how you feel now. Did you feel more connected? Did conversations go deeper? Did you experience less of an urge to check your device by the end of the week?

WHY THIS EXERCISE **MATTERS**

True belonging requires presence. When you practice being fully available to others, you activate your brain's dopamine system and invite a quality of relationships that is far more satisfying than hundreds of digital likes. ■

Embrace Vulnerability

One of the most underrated pathways to genuine connection is vulnerability—allowing yourself to be seen, struggles and all. When this is experienced in a positive way, dopamine is released, making that act of vulnerability rewarding while also encouraging you to put yourself out there in the future. This exercise builds your capacity for vulnerability, so your dopamine system—and your life—can reap the rewards.

1. **Identify one struggle, fear, or insecurity that you typically hide.** This could be a professional challenge, a personal worry, a shame story, or a need for support in a certain area of your life. Write about it honestly: What is it and why do you hide it?

2 **Choose one safe person to share this vulnerability with.** This should be someone who has demonstrated care and respect to you in the past. Plan to share your struggle with them in a specific conversation.

Who I will share with:

When and how I will share:

3 **Have the conversation.** Notice what happens when you risk vulnerability. How do they respond? Do you feel more connected? Does admitting the truth feel relieving or terrifying?

4 **Reflect on the shift.** In that moment of honest exchange, did you feel energized rather than depleted? Did you find yourself thinking about the person with warmth rather than anxiety? Did you want to continue the conversation rather than escape it? How did you feel afterward (more settled instead of agitated)? Did openness create safety and trust?

WHY THIS EXERCISE **MATTERS**

Vulnerability is not weakness; it is the gateway to genuine belonging. When you take this risk, dopamine becomes a signal of safe connection rather than a restless hunt for recognition. Over time, practicing vulnerability transforms how you relate to others and how they relate to you. It also strengthens those pathways in your brain that connect reward to engaging with others in meaningful ways. ■

Identify Who Supports Your Drive

Every person in your circle is a signal to your dopamine system. The people who motivate you strengthen the anticipation of reward that drives your next effort, while the people who drain you weaken it, sometimes before you even try.

1 **List three to five people you interact with most often right now.** These could be close friends, family members, colleagues, or anyone from a social group:

2 **For each person, ask yourself: "Do I feel more energized or more drained after time with them?"** Write your answers here:

3 **In addition to the people in your daily life, consider who inspires you from a distance.** Sometimes a writer, teacher, or creator you have never met can activate your dopamine system in ways that sustain long-term motivation. Identify one such person and note how their work affects your drive:

4 Plan one way to spend more time with the people you have identified. For example, consider a weekly check-in, a coworking session, accountability texts, or listening to their content before work. Write your plan here:

WHY THIS EXERCISE **MATTERS**

Supportive relationships make hard things feel more doable, and setbacks feel less final. When you intentionally lean into motivating connections, you give your dopamine system extra fuel to stay engaged. ■

Explore Where You Feel Isolated

Your dopamine system works best when it's connected to real, meaningful relationships. Without that, your brain tends to chase quick rewards—like scrolling through social media, overworking, or constant distractions—that don't actually satisfy you for long. This exercise helps you notice where connection might be missing so you can start building it back in intentionally.

1 **List the people you have meaningful contact with at least once per week.** These should be people with whom real conversation happens, not just transactional interactions:

2 **Using a scale of 1 to 10, rate the depth of each relationship.** With 1 being a surface-level relationship and 10 being a close, personal relationship (i.e., you feel deeply seen and understood by them), record your reflections here:

3 **Identify one area where you feel isolated or disconnected.** Is it at work? At home? In your neighborhood? In your sense of purpose?

Where I feel most disconnected:

4 Assess how you currently go about getting a sense of belonging. Do you have regular gatherings, celebrations, or shared practices with people you care about?

WHY THIS EXERCISE **MATTERS**

Connection cannot be assumed or taken for granted. By clearly seeing where you are isolated, you can start taking steps to create more belonging. In turn, your dopamine system will thrive. ■

Try Small Acts of Belonging

Deeper satisfaction is built on small, repeated practices that signal belonging to your dopamine system. This exercise helps you create rituals that will bring about connection.

1 **Choose one context where you want more connection.** This could be at the dinner table, in the workplace, in your neighborhood, or within your friend group or family.

The context:

2 **Design a small, simple ritual for this context.** This should take five to fifteen minutes and be repeatable. Examples include doing a gratitude circle with friends or asking a check-in question at the dinner table.

My ritual:

3 **Set a specific time and frequency.** Decide when this will happen.

Daily? Weekly? Monthly?

4 **Practice this ritual for the next four weeks.** Notice how it changes things in terms of connection, energy, and more.

After one week: How did it feel?

After two weeks: Any shifts in connection? If so, what?

After three weeks: How is it becoming a habit?

After four weeks: What has changed?

WHY THIS EXERCISE **MATTERS**

Small rituals are how you can build a stronger sense of belonging into your chosen communities. When dopamine is linked to predictable moments of connection and celebration, your brain learns to crave community rather than distraction. ■

Choose What Matters

Modern life often pushes people to always be doing, producing, and optimizing. What gets forgotten is presence: being with people in the moment and resting without feeling guilty about what you "should" be doing. Your dopamine system can end up so twisted around productivity that real connection feels like a waste—or isn't even on the radar. This exercise will help you evaluate whether your daily life prioritizes connection or mere productivity most.

1 **List your top five time commitments this week.** This can be work, family obligations, hobbies, entertainment, or admin tasks:

1. ______________________________

____

2. ______________________________

____

3. ______________________________

____

4. ______________________________

____

5. ______________________________

____

2 **For each one, ask: Does this serve genuine fulfillment, connection, or growth?** Or does it just take up your time?

____

____

____

____

____

____

____

____

____

____

3 **Identify one time commitment you could eliminate or reduce.** What would you gain by letting it go?

The commitment:

What I would gain by letting it go:

4 **Design one new practice to fill that space with genuine connection or purpose.** Examples include a weekly call with a close friend, a standing volunteer shift, a creative project that matters to you, a weekly walk with someone you care about, or a regular mentoring session.

My new practice:

WHY THIS EXERCISE **MATTERS**

Dopamine is most activated not when you are productive, but when you are present with people who matter. By digging into how you spend your time and making changes as needed, you ensure your daily life is actually fulfilling for you. ■

Turn "I" Into "We"

Individual Dopamine Menus are powerful, but dopamine truly flourishes in community. This exercise helps you design a practice that activates your satisfaction pathways on a group level.

1 **Identify one group you are part of or want to be a part of.** This can be a sports team, family, friend group, neighborhood, school, or organization.

The group:

2 **What is the shared purpose or identity of this group?** What could bring you together (e.g., a shared cause, a common tradition, or mutual support through life's transitions)?

Shared purpose/identity:

3 **Design one community ritual that honors this purpose.** This should activate dopamine for everyone involved. Examples include monthly gatherings, team celebrations, a neighborhood potluck, a book club, or a volunteer project.

The ritual:

4 **Plan how you will introduce and sustain this ritual.** Who will help? How will you communicate it? How will you keep it alive?

5 **After one month, reflect on the impact.** Did it deepen the sense of belonging? Did it shift the group's energy?

WHY THIS EXERCISE **MATTERS**

Life is fundamentally collective. When you introduce rituals that activate connection and celebration at the group level, you are not only rewiring your own reward circuits; you are also building communities where fulfillment is a shared practice rather than a solo pursuit. ■

Rewrite Your Story

If you have been impacted by trauma, one of the most powerful practices you can do to shape your dopamine system is deliberately reframing the narrative you tell yourself about that trauma. This is not about denying what happened; it is about consciously shifting focus to resilience and agency.

1 **Write the trauma story as you currently tell it.** How do you narrate what happened? What was your role? What do you think it means about you? Allow your honest story to emerge.

2 **Identify the limiting beliefs embedded in this narrative.** What does this story tell you about your worth, your capability, or your future? What beliefs keep you from moving forward?

3 **Now rewrite the story with a focus on your resilience and agency.** Keep the facts the same, but shift the lens. Where did you show strength? What did you learn? What became possible because of what you endured? Write a new version that honors the pain and acknowledges your capacity to survive and grow.

4 **Read your reframed narrative aloud daily for one week.** Notice if it lands differently in your body. Does it feel more true? Does it shift your sense of possibility? Reflect in the space provided.

WHY THIS EXERCISE **MATTERS**

The narrative you tell shapes your dopamine system and thus your motivation and your sense of possibility. By consciously reframing trauma as something that tested you but did not define you, you activate new brain pathways that shape your dopamine system around agency, hope, and resilience rather than helplessness, self-criticism, or other limiting beliefs. ■

Determine What Brings (or Blocks) Your Joy

If you completed the trauma exercises earlier in this workbook, this is where that awareness becomes a reclamation. Here, you will identify which sources of pleasure, if any, remain accessible to you after trauma and what barriers stand in the way of your joy.

1. **List activities, people, or moments that once brought you joy.** Think back to before the trauma. What lit you up?

2. **For each one, honestly rate how accessible that source of joy feels now.** Use a scale of 1 to 10, with 1 being not accessible at all and 10 being extremely accessible.

3 **Identify any new sources of comfort or safety that have emerged since the trauma.** Sometimes you can discover unexpected things that soothe you—a specific place, a person, or a practice introduced after trauma. If this sounds true for you, reflect on it here:

4 **Name one small pleasure that is currently accessible to you.** This does not need to be a lofty aspiration, but rather something that is genuinely achievable in the present moment.

One small pleasure I can access now:

WHY THIS EXERCISE **MATTERS**

Trauma dims dopamine. By identifying even tiny ways to activate it, you are finding the footholds to rewire your dopamine system. You are not trying to feel "happy" after the trauma; you are simply mapping where joy still exists, however small. ■

Commit to the Journey Ahead

This final exercise invites you to reflect on everything you have learned and commit to building a life—and helping build a community—grounded in genuine fulfillment.

1 **Reflect on your journey through this workbook.** What is the biggest shift in how you think about dopamine, motivation, and fulfillment?

2 **Identify your personal "non-negotiables" for fulfillment.** Based on what you have discovered in this workbook, what practices, rituals, or connections cannot be compromised going forward?

3 **Design your personal vision for the future.** What does your life look like when dopamine is aligned with purpose, connection, and genuine fulfillment?

4 **Commit to three specific actions this month.** These should be actions that build toward your vision.

Action #1	Action #2	Action #3

5 **Identify one person or group you want to inspire.** How can you model a life of dopamine balance for them?

WHY THIS EXERCISE **MATTERS**

By clarifying your commitment to fulfillment that is grounded in connection and purpose, you don't just hold yourself accountable to stay the course beyond these pages. You also become a living example of what is possible. Others will follow not because you convince them, but because they see your dopamine system working the way it was designed to work: toward genuine, shared flourishing. ■

EPILOGUE

Your Dopamine Code

You have now completed *The Dopamine Code Workbook*. You have learned about the science of dopamine, explored your habits and environments, designed rituals that align with your deepest values, and begun building practices that deliver genuine fulfillment.

But the work does not end here. In fact, it is just beginning. Every day, you have the opportunity to choose connection over distraction, purpose over productivity, and belonging over busyness. Every small ritual you introduce, every moment of presence you create, every celebration you share—these are important steps in keeping your dopamine system balanced and working for you.

As you move forward from this workbook, remember: Your dopamine system is not your enemy. It is your teacher, showing you what truly matters. Sustainable fulfillment is built through daily practices, not grand gestures. Continue using your Dopamine Menu and adjusting it whenever something else is needed or an item just isn't serving you anymore.

Also remember that you are not meant to do this alone. Genuine flourishing happens in community, through close relationships and also a greater sense of connection to the world around you. Bring others into your journey: Share what you have learned, and be open to what insights they might have.

The future you are building—through your choices, rituals, and relationships—is being written right now. Continue forward with intention, carry the tools you've built through this workbook, and watch your future unfold in amazing ways.

About the Author

Dr. Sydney Ceruto is a neuroscientist and the founder of MindLAB Neuroscience, where for more than two decades she has applied neuroscience to how people think, decide, and change. She holds a PhD in behavioral and cognitive neuroscience from New York University, and master's degrees in clinical psychology and business psychology from Yale University. She lectures in the Wharton Executive Development Program at the University of Pennsylvania. The pioneer of Real-Time Neuroplasticity™, Dr. Ceruto works closely with a small number of individuals at any one time to rewire the neural patterns behind their behaviors, decisions, and emotional responses. Her work has been featured in *Forbes*, *USA TODAY*, *Newsweek*, and *Business Insider*. She is the author of *The Dopamine Code* and its companion, *The Dopamine Code Workbook*.